Heels on Wheels

A lady's guide to owning and riding a bike

Heels on Wheels

A lady's guide to owning and riding a bike

Katie Dailey

Illustrations by Clare Owen

hardie grant books

MELBOURNE · LONDON

handlebar

brake
lever

front
light

Cross bar

brake

tyre

spokes

Crank

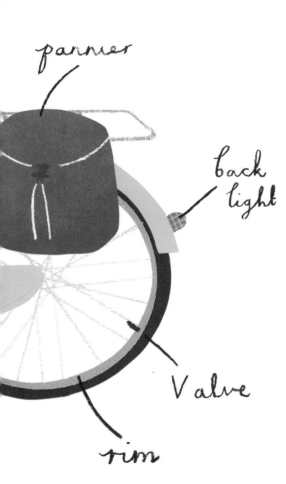

saddle

pannier

back
light

valve

rim

Contents

The bicycle is the most civilised conveyance known to man. Other forms of transport grow daily more nightmarish. Only the bicycle remains pure in heart.

Iris Murdoch

'It's amazing how I'm able to ride around on a bike. People kind of see it's me, but since I'm on a bike, they think, "No, it's not her". And by the time they realise it's me, I'm already gone.'

Beyoncé Knowles, entertainer extraordinaire

'The bicycle will accomplish more for women's sensible dress than all the reform movements that have ever been waged.'

Author unknown,
from **Demorest's Family Magazine**, 1895

'The bicycle is just as good company as most husbands and, when it gets old and shabby, a woman can dispose of it and get a new one without shocking the entire community.'

Ann Strong, **Minneapolis Tribune**, 1895

'Let me tell you what I think of bicycling.
I think it has done more to emancipate women
than anything else in the world. It gives women a feeling
of freedom and self-reliance. I stand and rejoice every
time I see a woman ride by on a wheel ... the picture
of free, untrammeled womanhood.'

Susan B. Anthony, 1820–1906, abolitionist and leader
of the American women's suffrage movement

Introduction

Having cycled around London – one of the most congested and overpopulated cities in the world – for over a decade amounts to thousands of hours spent fighting for space on the roads. I've had countless tussles with tarmac, narrowly missed an impromptu dip in a rancid canal, and been chased by really, really mean dogs. But I still don't know why anyone uses any other mode of transport to get anywhere. You don't realise how slow buses really are until you've been on a bike. Or how hot and claustrophobic a train or tube is until you've breezed through a park, framed by autumn leaves and the sound of birds chirruping in the trees. What is surprising is that in rush hour, when I pause for breath at a traffic light and look around at the other cyclists in the cycle lane, I'm almost always the only girl. There are plenty of ladies riding around at the weekend, pottering by the markets, but there are hardly any on the busy roads when there's traffic about. And there's certainly none when it starts to rain.

This book is designed to dispel any myths and fears surrounding cycling for the fairer sex, and will hopefully help you to avoid accidents, save your bike from thieves, and prevent you from turning up to work with helmet hair. Once you know what you're doing, cycling is one of the simplest, greatest pleasures of modern living, and everyone should be doing it. Especially girls. See you at the traffic lights!

Chapter 1

Getting Started

Why put your heel to the wheel?

If you've bought this book, chances are you're either considering getting a bike, or have just landed one. Welcome to the club – you've joined the ranks of Coco Chanel, Madonna, Vivienne Westwood and Jennifer Aniston (who was a bicycle courier in New York before finding fame as Rachel on *Friends*), not to mention a worldwide community of people who've discovered the enduring appeal of getting around on their own steam.

There are so many reasons why biking has survived the numerous advances in automotion – from motorbikes to scooters, cars to buses, and the fact that we're now competing with all of the above for road space. The foremost is the simple pleasure afforded by putting foot to pedal; cycling along with the wind in your hair and the sun on your face is extraordinarily enjoyable. There's no disputing that it's less fun in torrential rain, but one of the nicest things about cycling is that you can choose how much or little you do: fair-weather cyclist or die-hard, riding-in-all-elements fanatic.

Another key benefit of cycling is that you save both money and time (and stress!) by not using your car or public transport. Once you've made the initial outlay on the bike and gear of your choice, the financial upkeep should be fairly minimal. You can either maintain your bike yourself, using the maintenance guide on page 95 of this book, or you can factor into your budget a quarterly service at your local bike shop to keep your bike running smoothly and safely.

Time-wise, there's nothing more rewarding than being on your ride and gliding past traffic snarled up in jams. Cycling in cities is typically by far the fastest way of getting around. It's also easier to be punctual – once you've been cycling for a while you'll know roughly how long it'll take you to get anywhere, without having to factor in public transport delays or heavy traffic. You might also find that you have several different routes to the same destination – the scenic route through a park, where you can ride leisurely and enjoy the journey, or the more direct, busier route for when you need to get somewhere fast.

Cycling in the city

Five things to look out for when you're
cycling in the big smoke:

1. Potholes. With utilities companies continually digging up the
roads and not putting them back properly, potholes are the blight
of the streets. Avoid swerving quickly to miss them as someone
might be overtaking you. Sometimes it's safer to brake and ride
through them.

2. Rubbish trucks. Avoid cycling behind them at all costs as
the smell is unbearable – it's one of the most unpleasant
things a cyclist can endure. Dismount and overtake on the
pavement if necessary.

3. Crazy taxi drivers. If hailed by a potential customer, they pull
in and out with no warning. Give a wide berth.

4. Passengers alighting straight on to the road. Leave enough
space for an open door, or you could swoosh straight into one.

5. Inexperienced riders on hire bikes. The downside of hire
schemes is that they unleash a lot of people who don't know what
they're doing on the roads. Try to be patient with them, and avoid
touristy roads where hire stations tend to be installed.

Let it burn ... cycling for fitness

A glorious side-effect of cycling is that you're exercising without really noticing it. The contrast between sweating on a grubby running machine at a gym and winging your way through parks and leafy lanes on a bicycle is almost laughable – but the end results of the two aren't so different.

It's very hard to gauge how much energy you'll have burned at the end of a bike ride as there are so many factors to consider. Most online calorie calculators take into account the rider's weight as the key variant, but I'd place more emphasis on the quality of bike. Without stating the obvious, the better your bike, the less you'll be working as good ones, by their very nature, are designed to procure a favourable effort-to-distance ratio. As a very broad average:

- A medium-sized woman on a medium-quality bike cycling at an average speed will burn off around 500 calories an hour. If you do your sums, that equals a chocolate bar or a nice bottle of wine. Though do wait until you come to a stop!
- Make that a large woman on a heavy, slow bike with fairly flat tyres, cycling at twenty-three kilometres an hour, and you're looking at more like 1000 calories an hour.
- A tiny woman on a flash racer bike, encountering no hills and cycling leisurely at twelve kilometres an hour, is probably going to expend less than 250 calories. That doesn't even buy her a glass of wine and a bowl of peanuts.

The whole process of switching between standing and sitting positions as you ride is great for toning the legs and posterior, too – take a look at serious cyclists and they'll typically have lean lower legs with dauntingly muscular thighs. Need it be mentioned that Beyoncé is a keen cyclist!

So, all in all, cycling allows you to enjoy the endorphins and calorie-burning benefits of exercise whilst getting around quickly and cheaply.

First, establish what kind of cyclist you are

There are lot of ladies burning rubber out there. Taking to the wheel for the first time can be a scary prospect, and it's good to know who you'll be dealing with: the streets can be mean! Keep your eyes peeled for these cycle-lovers.

Fashion Victim

Fashion Victim tells people she's been cycling in the city 'since way back in the day'. In fact, she was a late adopter, happy on the trains and buses for years until she noticed snaps of Agyness Deyn cruising nonchalantly around New York on her vintage bike. Now she cycles everywhere on her neon-streaked fixie, built at great expense with parts from Japan – until she gets trashed at the pub, when she has to fake a flat tyre to persuade a taxi driver to allow her to squeeze in the back with her skinny, imported wheels.

Earth Mother

'Nonsense,' says Earth Mother when anyone expresses fears for the safety of her toddlers, one perched precariously on a seat at the rear of her rickety bike, the other sitting in a wire shopping basket that has been fastened fairly securely to the front. Nevertheless, she sticks to the main roads on the way to the farmer's market – leaving only a few petrified motorists to keep a firm eye on the infants dangling near their bonnets. 'My girls LOVE riding!' she exclaims, while behind her little Melody wistfully eyes a passing family wagon, and clings forlornly to the mudguard.

Speed Demon

Only the trained eye can identify the gender, or even species, of Speed Demon with any kind of confidence. With the application of technical fabrics and a terrifying helmet that looks like the eye of a devil from outer space, she has evolved into a species that is half-human, half-elongated beetle. Speed Demon's racer is worth more than a car, and her secret ambition is to clock the flash of a speed camera as she pummels her path along the dual carriageways that all other cyclists would fear to pedal.

Retro Rider

Retro Rider has no interest in anything manufactured since the birth of her grandmother. She is happy to ride a bicycle that weighs more than a cement-mixer, provided it looks aged, with brass fixtures that look like they have been procured from one of Alexander Graham Bell's prototypes. She cycles in laced-up chimney sweep's boots, the same shade of worn-in tan as her Brooks saddle, and carries paper bags of organic apples and second-hand books in her large, unwieldy basket. Hogging the cycle lanes with her jangling bike and clanging her copper bell, she is unaware of the queue of more speedy riders forming behind her, as she plucks an apple from her basket, and pictures herself whooshing across a Penguin Classics front cover.

Choosing a trusty steed

People who work in bike shops like to use confusing jargon when selling bikes; they probably don't even know they're doing it. Before buying, it's worth learning the basic differences between types of bike, as choosing the perfect ride isn't quite as simple as working out what looks good and fits your budget.

The first thing to be aware of is the weight of the frame. It might look good, but can you actually lift it? Remember there could be instances when you need to carry your bike up some stairs.

Riding a skinny-tyred road bike on gravel or cobbles is likely to knacker your wheels and, at least temporarily, threaten the well-being of your undercarriage. And riding a shopper on a long journey will take double the time of a whizzy racer. If a regular route involves hills, you will curse buying a fixed wheel every time you put foot to pedal – especially downhill, when your legs will run away with you and you'll probably end up flying half the way.

So, to enjoy your bike, it pays to think about where and how you intend to ride it. Most bike shops will allow you to have a test run, so take them up on this offer before you spend your hard-earned cash.

Your bike will fall into one (or sometimes two) of the following categories: mountain bike, single speed, fixed, upright/shopper or hybrid/city bike.

pepper's bikes

Mountain bikes

Anyone who has potholes, gravel, mud, grass or anything wobbly to ride over should opt for a mountain bike. No one could accuse them of having looks on their side, what with their big, craggy wheels and large, brash frames, but they're normally a very comfortable ride, absorbing all of the lumps and bumps that, on a city bike, could leave you walking like John Wayne for weeks to come. The point of them isn't speed, but cross-terrain resilience. It just comes down to how vain you intend on being.

Single speed

Single speeds are basically bikes with no gears. By getting rid of the gear mechanism, single speeds also get rid of half the hassles associated with riding – there's not much that can go wrong and you'll save money on gear tuning. Real bike geeks wouldn't have much to do with a single speed unless it was also a fixie (see page 28) but, unlike fixies, your speed is controlled by front brakes, which is comfortable, and they are a neat, nippy ride if you haven't got any hills to climb. Without gears, any big inclines will break you out into a sweat, but if you're in a flat city like London, Amsterdam or Sydney, it's a popular choice.

Fixed

Fixies, or track bikes, are built for speed. Literally. They were originally designed for track-racing on a wooden surface. Bike nerds consider these the purest form of ride, a gateway to a more visceral form of cycling because there's less intermediary between the legs and the wheel. They're also good for doing tricks (should you be that way inclined). Fixies are simply put together and let you regulate your speed with your legs rather than your brakes, and, as with single speeds, there's not much to break, which means low financial up-keep. On flat terrain and city rides, they are very pleasant – the bike pushes you as much as you push it, doing half the work for you. However, get to a downhill stretch and you'll quickly find your little legs pummelling the air, unable to slow down because your pedals are in sync with the wheels. That, combined with the pedal brake system, means that if you're a biking novice living at the top of a hill, they're probably not for you.

Upright/shoppers

As an entry-level bike, you can't really beat a shopper, or upright bike. Everyone knows how to ride them, and you can normally buy one cheaply or find one you'd forgotten you owned during your teenage years. Typically coming with a handful of brakes, they can be nippy if the chain is oiled, and they're normally nice and little so you can stow them in a hallway. You can easily fasten a basket to the front for loaves of bread, fluffy puppies and bunches of daffodils – and they look cute as hell. On the downside, they're typically creaky, with whiney brakes and rattling chains. Their fat little tyres also attract punctures and, if you have any further than about three kilometres to cycle, they're hopelessly slow. So, if you just want to trundle between shops on errands, like to look like you're in a period drama, and you don't mind going nowhere fast, then dig out the shopper in your dad's garage and you're good to go.

Hybrid/city bikes

These combine the features of mountain and road bikes to provide something ideal for city riding. They take their upright frame and flat handlebars from their mountain bike lineage, but have the lighter weight of a road bike. Their wheels have a wider mountain bike tread with higher road bike air pressure – meaning they can deal with potholes and the odd pavement jump, if you're feeling flash, but they're not as slow as a mountain bike on roads.

Get a handle on it: choosing your bars

You have probably never considered a handlebar in your life (unless questioning the strange resurgence of handlebar moustaches amongst hipsters). Your bike's handlebars can mean the difference between a smooth ride and a near-death experience. Check out the details below and make an informed decision.

Drop bars

These are the ones which look like rams' horns. They don't feel as natural as straight bars at first, as you have to hunch right over, but once you're used to drop bars, they give you much more bang for your pedalling buck due to the way they shift the position of the body.

Suicide bars

These are the very narrow, straight handlebars – so called because they encourage you to crunch yourself between the traffic. Gulp.

Cruiser bars

These are the large, curved bars you see on glider bikes – typically the ones for hire by beaches. They are quite unwieldy and are totally unsuitable for cities, but in open spaces they keep you upright with your arms outstretched so you can take in beautiful views.

Straight bars

These are fitted as standard on mountain bikes, shoppers and hybrids. You can lower them for a more sporty feel but, traditionally, they offer an upright position. They're easy to start off with, so perfect for the cycling novice.

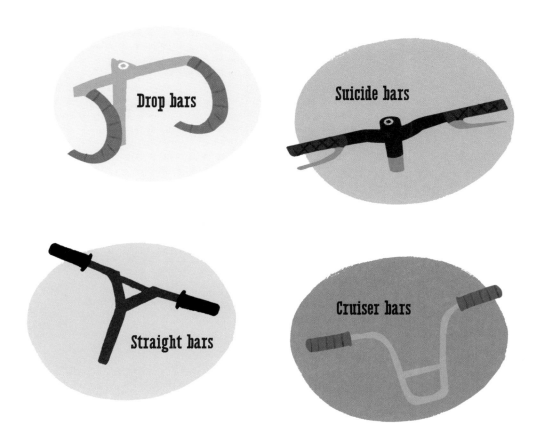

Drop bars

Suicide bars

Straight bars

Cruiser bars

Pain in the a*se

When your saddle isn't in the right position, it can feel like you have cracked your tailbone or sustained serious internal injuries. Get it really wrong, and you actually might, with the sensitive (and all-important!) perineum area most likely to come in for a bashing (or more precisely, a loss of feeling in the lady-bits department), potentially giving rise to a loss of sensation in an area that you'd probably quite like to hang on to. Saddles are one of the few biking components that are tailored specifically to each gender. So do buy one made for girls, as they're ergonomically designed to house ladies' bits rather than men's. Surprisingly, big, squashy seats aren't necessarily the most comfortable – the saddle that has given me least grief in a decade of city cycling is shaped like a stork's beak and is as hard as nails. It all depends on the position you cycle in.

Upright

Because your weight is shifted to the back of the seat, you'll typically want a wide, cushioned or gel-filled saddle. Girls tend to require a wider seat than boys as they have a broader pelvis.

Forward bias (seat as or nearly as high as handlebars)

You'll still want some padding at the rear of the saddle, which should be about the width of your sitting bones. But go for something narrow at the nose, so it doesn't rub your thighs.

Racer/hunched

If you ride with your seat high, and your elbows low, you'll need a narrow saddle – ideally with a cut-out or softened portion at the rear centre.

Tip

Positioning of your saddle

Take care to position your seat high enough (few do – your toes should only really graze the ground with your legs straight). And regularly check that your saddle hasn't been knocked off kilter. This can be very often if someone has unsuccessfully tried to relieve you of your saddle, then it can be left slightly askew. If it sits even a very few millimetres off-centre, you can have an uncomfortable ride.

Ultimate she-cycles

Now that you've decided what sort of bike best suits your lifestyle, you just need to buy it – the fun bit! It's a good idea to try a bike before buying it, to make sure it's comfortable. Your local bike shop is a good place to start, along with the websites listed in the Resources section on page 108.

A key thing to remember is that the main point of difference between bikes for boys and girls is that on cheaper models there's a lower cross-bar, so you can clamber over easily while wearing a skirt. In all other respects, apart from the pretty colours, the distinctions are few – the cross-bar might be a bit shorter to allow for a smaller torso, and there's likely to be a wider saddle for women's seat bones (although you can easily replace a saddle on a man's bike). However, there has recently been a spate of bikes designed with the feminine aesthetic particularly in mind. These include the Pashley, the Brompton, as well as several models from large fashion houses including Chanel and Gucci!

Buying a second-hand bike

The first thing you need to try and do is make sure the bike you have your eye on isn't stolen. Is it a £500 bike being sold for £50? It's stolen. Is it a short man selling a massive frame? It's stolen. Ask a few questions about the bike and how it rides. If the vendor looks nonplussed then it's probably been nicked. Stolen bikes are bad Karma, so avoid them at all costs.

Don't be fooled into thinking a cheap bike is automatically a good bike because you haven't had to shell out a large lump sum. Remember that even if it's only the wheels need replacing, you can automatically triple the price of the bike.

Give the bike a really throrough inspection. Start by looking at the parts which are most expensive to replace. Turn the bike upside down and spin the wheels – they should spin freely and then come to a natural stop. If they don't, the bearings might've gone.

Next, pull the chain away from the chain ring. If there's a lot of give, then you might have to invest in a new chain set. Have the teeth of chain set worn into a sharkfin shape? This might also mean an expensive replacement.

Cheaper parts to repair and replace are the brakes, handlebar tape and seats (which can often be found for a steal at car boot sales and markets), so don't be put off by these minor defects.

Do have a little test run before you commit to anything. Is the bike the right size? Is it the right weight? Is it light enough to carry up to your flat if you live on the second floor? Check the seat post is adjustable – sometimes they're rusted into position, making them useless if they're stuck at the wrong setting.

If you're not confident looking for defects, take a friend who is, otherwise you'll buy something unsuitable and have to look for a new bike in a week's time.

> When the spirits are low, when the day appears dark, when work becomes monotonous, when hope hardly seems worth having, just mount a bicycle and go out for a spin down the road, without thought on anything but the ride you are taking.

Sir Arthur Conan Doyle, creator of Sherlock Holmes and avid bike enthusiast

Chapter 2

How To Incorporate Cycling Into Your Lifestyle

Cycle chic

Don't let the fear of turning up to work or a night out looking a mess put you off incorporating cycling into your regular routine. A bit of wind-swept hair and an excessively dewy forehead are hard to avoid whatever the weather, but wearing the right clothes to cycle in can help you ride comfortably, arrive presentably and, most importantly, in one piece. Having been thrown over handlebars due to stray bag straps and laces, and negotiated an entire London Fashion Week by bike, I can confidently say being prepared and well-attired makes all the difference.

Make-up

Whether cruising on the weekend or flooring it to work, it's essential to wear lots of lip-salve and a good moisturiser to protect your skin from the elements. You'll also need a sunscreen on your nose all year round if you're going to cycle a lot.

CITY BLOCK
SPF 40

BAD lash

HOOLA

There isn't that much point in putting on a full face of make-up before you ride, unless your journey is short and leisurely, but ladies who do love to put a face on, do not be put off! If you wear foundation, go for a mineral-based powder or bronzer so that your skin can breathe, and won't be a magnet for insects and dirt. For the same reasons, glossy, sticky lip-glosses should be avoided – a fly getting trapped in your high-gloss lips is not conducive to that come hither look, and your hair getting stuck on your face can cause temporary blindness. Play up your eyes as much as you like and add a finishing dust of powder and lippy once you arrive at your destination.

How to arrive at work looking polished

Tips

1. Buy a big pack of baby wipes to keep at your desk. You can use them to quickly freshen up your post-perspiration bits or to get the odd bit of bike grease off your hands.

2. Blotting papers are a useful extra to keep in a desk drawer to quickly take off any post-cycling glow before you go into a meeting.

3. Allow an extra five or ten minutes to your journey, so you can cycle leisurely and arrive serenely.

Helmets

No one likes helmets – except maybe paramedics. They're uncomfortable. They make your head sweat and your hair flat. They're also life-savers, and it really is silly to cycle without one. Fortunately, there is a new generation of helmets that make you look less like you're about to be shot out of a cannon – even Marc Jacobs designed his own range last year with peaked tweed covers.

For your modern-day cycling girl, there are two main types to choose from: hard shell – a foam shell with a plastic cover; and soft shell – a foam shell with a fabric cover. While style is important, you should also be looking out for the safety standards that it conforms to. There's no point getting something that looks good if it doesn't work!

Things to keep in mind when choosing your helmet

- Ventilation is good (sweaty head is not).

- Can you see properly with it on? Hindered vision is a no-no, even if it looks really good.

- It should be a good fit. Ask a shop assistant to advise you on this.

- Avoid anything too heavy: it'll quickly make your neck ache.

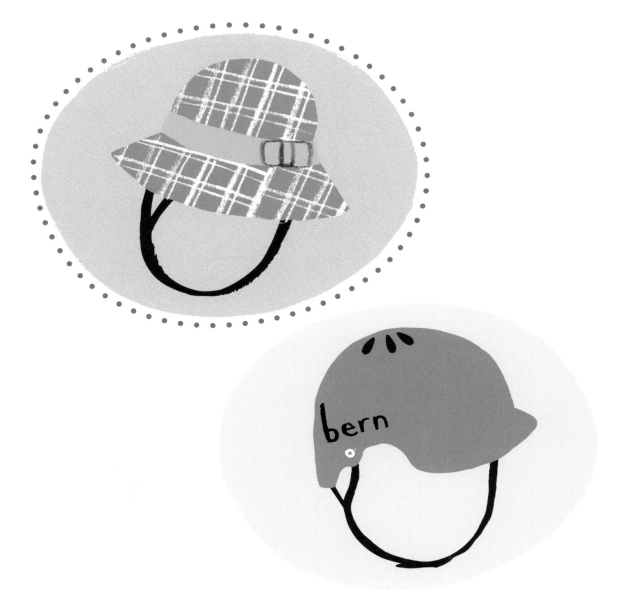

- If it's comfortable you're more likely to wear it.
- Ditto if it's stylish.

The most coveted ones are neat, small and shiny; look for internationally stocked styles from Bern, Schwinn and Sawako Furuno (they come in leopard print).

However, be warned that what you gain in style you lose in air-conditioning – the big, ugly styles in the traditional teardrop shape have much better air circulation than the new, compact shapes. So if you're going for the long haul, go for something sporty with big cut-out chunks and plenty of padding from a trusted brand like Giro. For maximum effect, don't wear anything underneath your helmet, and always strap it on before getting on your bike.

Sunglasses

Never has there been a better excuse to invest in a pair of expensive shades. Your favourite specs will not only protect your eyes from the elements (dirt, rain and cyclists' blight – the insect community), they'll also cut out the glare – thus minimising the risk of ghastly crows' feet – and inject an extra element of class and sophistication to your cycling attire. If you're short-sighted, it can be more comfortable to wear prescription sunglasses than specs.

Gloves

Do not leave home without them, unless it is sweltering outside. The cold seems to be visited upon the extremities with particular force when you're riding, so get fleece-lined ones for extra protection in winter, and down-size to lightweight leather ones for warmer months. Ignore the people who suggest fingerless gloves for cycling – the tips of your fingers are exactly the bits you're trying to keep cosy.

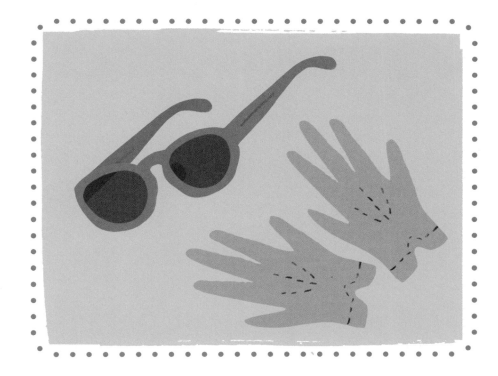

Reflective gear

Reflective gear is a useful extra. It doesn't have to be a big jacket. Fluorescent gilets are very cheap and portable, and slip on over your outfit or coat easily. Nor does it have to be designed for cycling – brands like American Apparel make cool waterproof hoodies in lots of fluorescent colourways. If you don't want to wear reflective clothing (who does?), you can fashion fluorescent vests into a rucksack cover – or even better, buy reflective rucksack cover. Alternatively, reflective Velcro bands are quick and easy to tape around trouser legs and wrists.

Waterproofs

Cycling is definitely a fair-weather friend, but if you dress properly it can be done in all seasons. The key to dressing in the cold is to wear several thin layers rather than a couple of thick ones, and to keep your hands, feet and neck very warm. The most important thing is your waterproof. There's nothing worse than heading off in the sunshine and not being able to get home at the end of the day due to a pesky drop of rain. A traditional plastic mac, that you'd wear to a festival, is not suitable for cycling though, as it acts like a sweat-box.

It's worth investing in a cycling jacket, similar to those worn by runners. They have ventilation under the arms and at the back of the neck, and are made of a special 'wicking' material which 'wicks' out sweat, helping you to stay warm and dry. They also scrunch up

into a little pouch or pocket so no one needs to see them once you dismount.

A myth perpetuated by cycle fashion websites is that capes make good cycling wear. Anyone who has tried to force a wodge of cape material through rucksack straps knows this not to be the case! Do not be fooled: the cape is not your friend.

If you are wearing a winter coat, take out the belt as it's likely to get caught in your spokes. Likewise scarves, which are prone to unravelling, and snaking their way into wheels to disastrous effect. A snood or neck-warmer will make cycling in cold weather infinitely more comfortable. A good rule of thumb is to set off feeling slightly chilly – you'll warm up as you cycle along. If you start off warm enough, you'll quickly get too hot.

Skirts

Long ones get caught in your spokes, tight ones can only be worn when hitched up to your waist, and pencil skirts mean you can't move your knees properly. The ideal skirt or dress is to the knee and not too flimsy. Wear something flyaway and it will do just that, rendering you temporarily blind and other road users dazzled by your knickers. And while tying your skirt may seem like a good idea at the time, the untie, once you have reached your destination, can leave you looking like a crumpled mess. You have been warned ...

Trousers

The best trousers for cycling are obviously leggings or anything with a bit of stretch. You'll need to tuck baggier trouser legs into your socks, or roll them up to prevent them catching on your chain. Totally unsuitable are very skinny jeans with no stretch, and anything low slung – the moment you lean forward you'll be exposing the people behind you to a full moon. If you go low, wear a long top to compensate. And if you're feeling daring, dabble with some shorts or even a romper/playsuit – they give you lots of room to manoeuvre.

Cycling shorts

Don't stop reading! Cycling shorts are unquestionably awful – left in the 1980s with very good reason, EXCEPT when actually cycling. The proper ones come with padding at the crotch, but are a slimline shape that means they're easy to pull on under skirts, baggy shorts or even jeans. Comfort wise, if you've got a long journey on the cards, you'll be grateful of a pair of cycling shorts on your legs.

Shoes

It's a sad truth that most proper cycling shoes, the ones that clip onto specially made pedals, look a bit like badgers. If you get serious about cycling, or have a long commute, they make you faster and save energy, but damn, they know how to kill a good outfit and are almost impossible to walk in when you dismount. Wear them on the bike, but not at home, kids.

The easiest shoes to cycle in are good-quality plimsolls with bendy, thick soles, and without dangly laces. Remember those curly elastic laces you used to be able to get before you could tie your own shoes? Aesthetically, they completely miss the mark, but they are perfect for cycling. Ballet pumps are easy to ride in at first, but aren't tough enough for long trips, and they'll lose their looks if you subject them to too many journeys. The ideal thing is to stow a pair of rubbery, laceless plimsolls in your bag for riding.

However, when you do find yourself with only a pair of heels, you wouldn't be the first person to ride in them completely happily. No one would recommend it from a safety point of view – the heel can jerk off from under you and make you swerve – but if you're going to do heels on wheels, make them stacked or wedged. When wearing your heel, use the ball of your foot and toe area rather than wedging your heel onto the pedal. It's slightly more difficult to ride like this, but will at least save you from ripping off a heel mid-cycle.

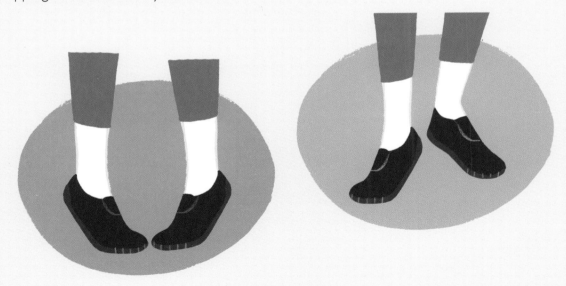

Don't sweat the small stuff

- If you don't have somewhere at work to shower and change, the deleterious effects of cycling on personal appearance can be quite off-putting. To be honest, the hassle of squeezing on and off public transport can be equally as dishevelling, but you can minimise the old helmet-hair/greasy trouser cuff syndrome: wear an airy helmet and tie your hair back.

- If you make one concession to cycle-wear, make it proper sports leggings. They come as calf-length and full-length versions, depending on how cold it is. You can change in the loo and squeeze them into a small bag when you get to your destination.

- Don't wear a traditional anorak – these act like sweat-boxes and don't offer any ventilation. Invest in a proper lightweight aertex jacket with netting under the arms.

- Keep antiperspirant on your back and chest as well as underarms.

- Wear cotton knickers and tights rather than nylon ones.

- On cold days, wear cool, light layers rather than thick ones, keeping thicker fabrics for hands and feet.

- Keep a little pack of wet wipes, or a mini soap or shower gel to hand. That way you can sneak into the loos and have an Italian shower, if not a real one.

- Keep a set of disposable gloves in your puncture repair kit for repairs.

Pimping your ride

Lights

When you're next out at night, have a look for the cyclists without lights on. You need cat's eyes to see them; night cyclists without lights are invisible, and you'd be mad to put yourself on the road lightless at a time when most drivers are not at their most alert. Go for lights with a 'blink' setting, as static lights can just blend into the nighttime landscape. Like cars, put the white one on the front, red on the back. And always put them in your bag when you lock up your bike outside, as they're easy to detach and steal.

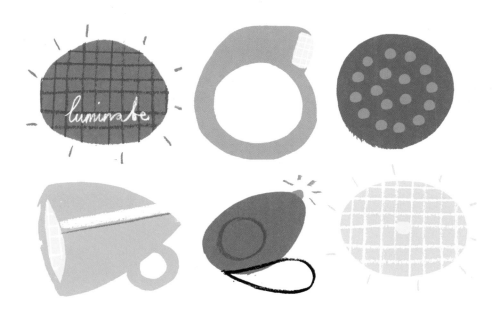

Pannier, bag or basket?

If you have a bike that you can affix a pannier or basket to, you absolutely should, as cycling with a rucksack is a pain in the back, while shoulder bags slip off into spokes easily. The advantage of panniers is that they're tucked down by your wheels, so it's less likely that thieves will be able to probe into them. Not everyone can fix them to their bikes – you'll need a frame to clip them to, which doesn't really work on racers. If you are going for panniers, do get two, as one means you're riding off-balance. Also, don't underestimate how much heavier a full pannier or two will make your bike. I've capsized on one side due to the sheer weight of my panniers, ending up like an upturned beetle, unable to get up again. Not cool.

Baskets are useful and look lovely, they're easy to plonk a bag into, and don't get in the way. They're also very easy for thieves to reach into, grab said bag, and make a speedy getaway. If you plan to keep your bag in it while you ride, use even the most basic of locks to fasten your bag to it.

Bells, bells, bells

A bell may seem like a non-essential bike
accessory, but there's no better way to warn
pedestrians of your approach than by saluting
them with a friendly ding, especially when looping
round bendy canals when you can't see each other coming.
They're also very easy on the eye.

Tips

Accessorising your bike

Accessorising your bike can become an expensive habit, so look
out for bits and bobs at car boot sales and flea markets – more
often than not you'll find cheap bike lights and old saddles to
have a play with. Tinkering about with your ride can become a
surprisingly satisfying pastime (and it's easy to justify spending
money on a vehicle that saves you so much time and cash!).

Chapter 3

Cycling Safely

Be visible

The key way to be safe on the road as a cyclist is to be as visible and assertive as you possibly can. Recent studies have suggested women are more likely to get hit on the roads because we cycle prudently and unassertively – tucking ourselves into the pavement where we can't be seen and hanging back at traffic lights. Basically, to improve our chances on the road, we need to man up. Position yourself at the front of the traffic at lights and never, EVER pavement hug when it comes to a turn as you simply won't be seen by big vehicles turning left. Be decisive in your movements and clearly signal your intentions. It is better to be irritating and in the way, than under the wheel of a bus.

You also need to be aware of motorists' blind spots. A blind spot is the area of the road that cannot be seen while a driver is looking through the rear or side mirrors of a car. Keep away from these spots at all costs.

In terms of biking gear, throw all your usual sartorial rules out of the window and wear clothing as bright and brash as you can possibly muster – and when it comes to cycling in the dark, turn your bike into a mobile rave with lights and fluoro fabrics to avoid becoming a thing that goes bump in the night.

Cycle school

The A, B and Cs of riding

As the well-worn adage goes, it's the one thing you never forget. However, cycling in a city or on major roads is a far cry from trundling round your parents' garden with stabilisers on. If you're quietly nervous about taking to the pedal again, check to see if your local council is running any cyclist training courses. These are a great way to gain some confidence before hitting the open road, which can be quite daunting.

Many governments across the world now offer handbooks that are specifically aimed at cyclists, and can be downloaded for free off the Internet – see the Resources section on page 108 for more details. In the meantime, here are some tips to help you cycle confidently, and safely, in the big smoke.

Keep left until you near a junction. But leave enough width for people in parked cars to unexpectedly open their doors without knocking you senseless.

Ignore anyone who beeps at you for keeping your distance from cars, or if you're moving towards the middle of the road to take a turn. Remember that, in effect, every cyclist represents a car taken off the road, so cars should be happy that you're there, freeing up a bit of road for everyone else.

On the subject of beeping, it is a loathsome fact of a girl's cycling life that men will pull up in trucks right behind her while she pedals, then issue a deafening honk of their horn to signal their appreciation. Why a certain breed of man feels that to scare you witless and burst your eardrums is tantamount to a kind of mating ritual, is hard to fathom, but there is little to be done about it.

Plan your route before setting off. The quickest route isn't always the safest. Try to go for the quieter roads, or ones with bicycle lanes.

Do be considerate of motorists though. If it's hard for a car to pass you, pull in when you can to let them overtake. Always signal when you're about to turn (practise keeping your balance in the park), and do put your lights on so they can see you. Most drivers live in terror of hurting a cyclist, and most cyclists are pretty selfish on the road – leading to a highway impasse that helps no one.

Don't take for granted that any driver knows what they're doing though. Never assume a motorist has looked in his/her wing mirrors; they might not have. When cycling alongside white vans, try to make fleeting eye contact with the driver so you can be sure they've seen you.

When you reach a junction, do NOT stay left. Move to the front of the traffic on your side of the road, and stay in the middle until you have a chance to go. It might make you feel vulnerable to move from your default left position, but it is absolutely the safest thing to do. All the cars behind you can see you if you're up front centre. The most dangerous place a cyclist can be is left of a truck. Most of them literally can't see you – which is why nearly all the ghost bikes (white bikes left at the site of a cyclist mortality) in cities are to be found on junctions.

Consider your shoulders your wing mirrors. Check over them every time you make a move – even if you're pulling out to the right of a lane of traffic – and don't expect anyone to have room to overtake you. There's always a speeding pizza delivery man on a motorbike with a death wish who can come out of nowhere.

Beware buses. Buses believe (and in some cities they are absolutely right) that they have the right of way over the flow of traffic they are about to turn into. If you are cycling alongside a bike lane, bear in mind that a bus could pull out and mow you down in a nanosecond.

Keep to the backstreets wherever you can. It sounds obvious but, as well as being safer, they afford a much more pleasurable journey – and backstreets have much fewer traffic lights.

Don't cycle when it's icy or snowy. Aside from the horrid biting coldness of it all, icy roads are a death trap for cyclists – particularly for those on skinny wheels.

Try not to brake suddenly as you could easily fly over your handlebars. Instead, apply your back brake first, followed by your front, so that you come to a gradual halt. Landing face-first on the pavement is *so* not cool.

Avoid doing anything that makes you feel uncomfortable (within reason). If your planned route takes you through a multi-lane roundabout and the mere thought scares the hell out of you, take the backstreets.

Be aware that some medications can impair your decision-making skills. Cycling blind drunk isn't much better than drink-driving – and no one thinks that's a good idea. You can probably get away with a bit more booze at the handlebars than behind the wheel, but bear in mind that in some countries and states of America, cycling drunk gets points docked off your driving licence (if you have one, this is incredibly annoying). Most bikes fit into the back of a cab, all bikes fit on a train carriage, and one of the most important things about knowing how to cycle is knowing when not to cycle.

Chapter 4

Parking (Or, How To Ensure Your Bike Isn't Stolen)

Thievery corporation

Theft is the blight of biking. In the UK alone, **a bike is stolen every minute** – and that is only counting the crimes that are reported, which is believed to be only around a third of the total. If a thief really, **REALLY wants your bike**, he'll find a way to get it. How will he steal your ride? Six Machiavellian thievery techniques:

1. The bolt

2. The glue sticker

3. Cut out the middle-man

4. First past the post

5. Basket case

6. Get wheel

> I got my bike stolen as a kid. When you're that age, it's one of the worst things in the world to wake up in the morning and not see your bike where you left it.

Curtis Jackson III, also known as rapper and general tough guy 50 Cent

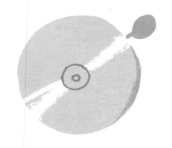

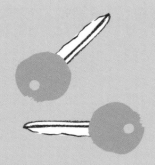

1. The bolt

- Thief arrives with bolt-cutters in bag and kneels to shield his fiendish activity from sight.
- Thief quickly snips the chain (with bolt-cutters, it's like cutting a blade of grass).
- Thief stashes broken chain and bolt-cutters in his bag, jumps onto your bike and whizzes away. To the casual observer, it will have looked like a quick unlock.

2. The glue sticker

- Thief disables your lock (often by filling the slot with glue, the little blighter) so that you can't release your bike, thereby forcing you to leave it overnight while you figure out a solution.
- Thief waits for the small hours, when he is left free to break your lock open, unobserved, at a leisurely pace.

3. Cut out the middle-man

- Thief is stumped by your sturdy lock, so he targets the material it is affixed to. Rickety posts, grates and wire are sitting ducks when he is armed with a saw or bolt-cutter.
- Thief lifts bike off with lock still attached. If you have locked only your frame, and not a wheel, he can cycle with the lock dangling obscenely in the wind.

4. First past the post

- Thief encounters your bike securely locked to a post with a small street sign at the top.
- He can either un-screw the sign or, if he's got height or a box on his side, slide it off over the top end. (NB this does not work on lamp posts).

5. Basket case

- In order to protect your handsome new basket from prying hands, you have locked your basket to the lamp post or bike rack. This pleases thief. Thief unfastens your basket from your bike.
- Thief is now able to undo your basket and leave it dangling from its post, still locked, while he trundles off on your bike.

6. Get wheel

- You have locked your bike through the wheel to prevent your wheel being stolen. This pleases thief. Thief uses an alum key to release your wheel from the frame.
- Thief detaches the frame from the locked wheel, throws your bike over his shoulder into his dastardly van, and drives away, leaving your locked wheel forlornly attached to its post and looking sorry as hell.

If there's one piece of advice you should consider over all others when considering bike security, it is this:

BUY a D-lock

Nothing else really poses any kind of opposition to thieves. It is worth considering a lock an investment that you'll keep for years to come, even as you upgrade your bike. Don't flinch at spending up to three figures if you can; you won't regret it. Good gold-standard D-locks come with their own insurance, meaning that if they fail you, the manufacturer will buy you a new bike. This in itself saves you money.

The safest locks you can buy are probably from Kryptonite's New York 'Fahgettaboudit' range, named after the world's bike-theft capital.

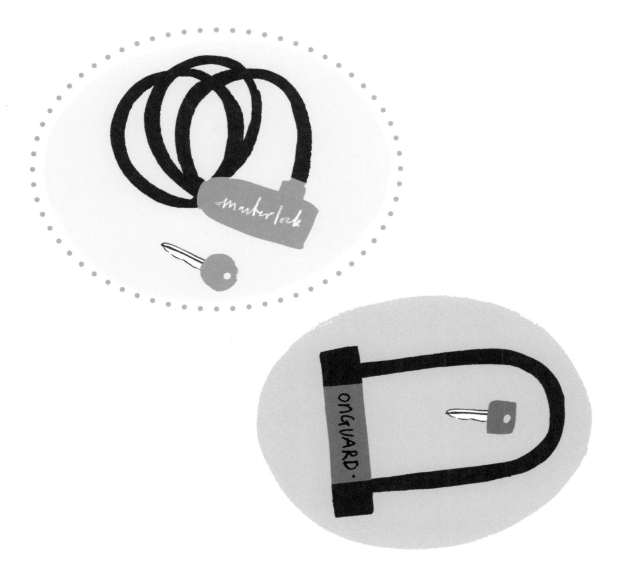

And the rest...

It's also a common irritation to find your joy at discovering your bike where you left it tempered when you realise it has been relieved of its various components, from seats to handlebars and wheels. I once had my brakes stolen from my bike – which struck me as singularly unkind. It's worth remembering that insurance rarely covers you for the loss of individual parts, only the bike as a whole. Often, the cost of a good saddle and wheel equals the worth of the frame, so it's worth ensuring that the amount of money you spend on keeping your bike intact is greater than the sum of its parts.

- Pit locks are brilliant. You can use these to replace the easily removable nuts and bolts or quick releases that keep your bike together, making it very hard for thieves to make off with bits of your bike you'd rather they didn't – a wheel, say, or a saddle. You need to carry around a special spanner in case you get a puncture and need to remove a wheel, but it's worth it, knowing that the thieves are unlikely to have one on them.
- If you're definitely happy with your saddle height, and don't plan to grow or shrink (or sell your bike), then glue your seat-post into position.
- Lock your bike through both your front wheel and frame, never one or the other.
- If your frame is expensive, tape or paint over it – it's heartbreaking to muss up its good looks, but the process makes your expensive bike less identifiable to thieves.
- Register your frame with local police so that you can prove it's yours when you

spot it being ridden by the local bike scoundrel after you locked it by the pub.

- Use two different locks: one a D-lock, the other a different type. It takes different tools to break different locks and it's unlikely thieves will carry a full arsenal.
- Buy locks that fit close to the frame, without leaving room for bolt-cutters to get any leverage.

If this sounds like too much bother and slightly hysterical, look up bike theft on YouTube. It's terrifying how little time and effort it takes to steal a bicycle.

If you want to find your bike where you left it, and not entrust it to the care of covetous cycle-thieves, try to look for the following:

- A pole or rack that is fixed securely to the ground. Sounds obvious, but a lot of lamp posts are much less secure than they look. Give it a big rattle before you lock your precious cargo to it.
- A place in plain view of passing footfall and traffic.
- Poles too high for a bike to be lifted over the top.

Avoid:

- Leaving your bike anywhere overnight – a lot of thieves operate during the small hours when there's less footfall.
- A place next to parking spaces wide enough for a van. Thieves often pull up in them, use them to shield devilish thievery, then whip your bike in the back.
- Outside pub gardens where all the clientele are asked to go inside at a certain hour. As soon as the shutters close, the thieves (who know exactly when the lock-in regularly begins) descend.

Insurance

Insurance is relatively cheap, and the cheaper your bike, the cheaper insurance is. If you live in a city, bike theft is sadly very much par for the course, so insurance is a great idea and means, however much you love your bike, you'll only be temporarily inconvenienced when it inevitably goes.

Unlike most car policies, bike insurance companies typically offer new for old, so if you bought and insured a brand new Colnago in 2004, you'll get a brand new Colnago in 2012 when you claim. Take photos of your bike for insurance purposes. Most bikes have a unique serial number (closely inspect your frame and keep a note of it). If there isn't one, you can always get one done. This could make it easier to trace your stolen frame.

Insurance doesn't just cover theft; what if you're involved in an accident and it's your fault? You could be liable for damaging someone else's property. It's a good idea to keep this in mind when taking out a policy. It's awful to not only be injured, but to be out of pocket, too.

You didn't hear it from us, but if you're making a claim for a bike that was stolen at night, it won't hurt to say it was taken before 9 pm, as many policies don't cover bikes left out overnight. Also, never try to claim for a bike stolen from inside your house; they're rarely covered as it overlaps with house insurance. Do check your house insurance though, as you could be covered for bikes under that – even whilst out and about.

> *I thought of that while riding my bike.*

Albert Einstein on the Theory of Relativity

Chapter 5

'Just One Last Question ...'

– all the answers you sought,
but felt too daft to ask

Is there any cycling etiquette I need to be aware of?

Not really – just be mindful of other road users. While you have every right to be on the road, you shouldn't take over it. If you're slow, and you know it, be courteous and let other cyclists and motorists pass you when there's a gap to pause in. Although it's nice to chat to a friend while you ride, if there are cars behind you then pull into single file so they can overtake. And try to use your body in place of the lights and signals you find on cars – waving cars on, pointing and gesticulating (in a decent fashion) to show people your next move.

Can I give a friend a lift/dink/backie?

Oh, we've all done it – perched on the saddle while an obliging friend wheezes at the pedals, on a bicycle decidedly not made for two. It's a bit dumb, and you'll probably fall off, so stick to parks and lanes as they're easier to fall on. Be warned – as well as being uncomfortable, slow and a bit dangerous, backies can almost guarantee a flat tyre or a buckled wheel if you stick at them for long enough. They're so exhausting, however, it's unlikely you'll be at it enough time to cause much damage to you or your bike.

How can I transport my dog on my bike?

Some cyclists have dogs fast enough to keep pace, even on a lead, with their cycling. If yours is of the small, cuddly and a little bit lazy variety, you can find baskets with protective cages over them to keep your pet in position. These are good for peace of mind when you ride, as even the idlest of dogs can be wont to leap from their places if they're distracted by bitches and butcher shops.

Can I talk on the phone/listen to music while riding?

Strictly speaking, no. You're already without the mirrors and lights motorists have to keep them aware on the road – your ears, together with your eyes, keep you aware of what's ahead and behind you. If you're going to wear headphones, go for the worst you can – the ones that don't block out sound, so you can still hear the traffic. Keep volume low, and only wear in one ear.

What's this I hear about saddle sores?!?

Relax: unless you're cycling an awful lot in a terrible saddle, saddles sores are unlikely to happen. If you are one of the unlucky ones, keep off your bike for a while, keep your sore bits clean with an antiseptic soap, and apply an over-the-counter acne gel containing 10% benzoyl peroxide. As ever, if the problem is ongoing, seek your doctor's advice.

I don't have a basket or panniers: can I hang shopping off my handlebars?

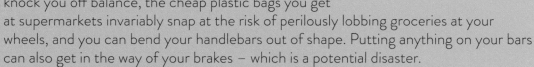

If you're very, very confident on your bike, and you have straight handlebars, it can be a quick fix on the way home. It's really not advisable, though, as it can knock you off balance, the cheap plastic bags you get at supermarkets invariably snap at the risk of perilously lobbing groceries at your wheels, and you can bend your handlebars out of shape. Putting anything on your bars can also get in the way of your brakes – which is a potential disaster.

What should I do if I have an accident?

First of all get off the road. If you have had a knock on the head, or feel sore anywhere, get someone to take you straight to hospital. Even if you feel fine, you might have concussion, which you should definitely have looked at. If you've damaged someone else's car, you might need to check with your insurance company if they'll help out with any culpability. If someone has damaged you or your bike, you can seek compensation, and a quick internet search will find agencies specialising in cycle law.

Can I cycle while knocked-up?

The risk of being injured while pregnant is just as great, but no greater than when you don't have a baby on board. Lots of women opt not to, as they are nervous of damaging their precious cargo – but provided you cycle carefully and slowly (the extra weight you're carrying might mean it takes longer for your brakes to kick in when cycling at speed), the exercise can be a good thing. Just keep well hydrated, and don't let the absent-mindedness some women complain of while pregnant affect your recollection to check on signals and traffic.

Should I run the red lights?

Everyone knows you shouldn't; an awful lot of people do (in London, even the mayor was caught doing it). As well as getting to where you're going quicker, nipping through a red light can give you a head start on the traffic behind you, particularly useful on a left turn. However, no-one should be doing it, as red lights are there to give priority to road users and allow them to take turns – and it's illegal. If you're spotted doing it, you'll be charged or fined.

Do I need to hand signal? I don't see all bike riders doing it.

Sometimes you can make it very obvious you're about to turn left by looking over your shoulder, pulling right into the kerb and swinging round. Hand signals do no harm (if you've perfected your one-arm balance) and an awful lot of good – anything you can do to keep your neighbouring motorists up to speed on your road plans is worth doing. Practise in the park to make sure you can do it steadily.

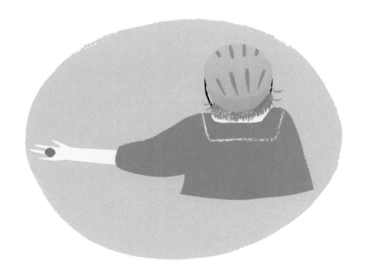

Can I ride in the rain or snow?

Rain – yes, just check your brakes before you leave as it can make them less grippy. Snow – no. Never.

Can I ever cycle on the pavement?

No – it's not normally legal, it's frightening for pedestrians, and there's no real reason to do it. Find quiet roads if you're worried about traffic – leave the pavements to the bipeds.

What's the deal with all the cycle schemes popping up across the globe?

These are proof that the world is coming round to the idea that cycling is brilliant and everyone should be doing it.

Barcelona has an excellent city-wide hire scheme, sadly open only to residents, but Paris, London, Dublin, Shanghai, Beijing, Milan, Brussels Hangzhou and over ninety cities across the globe have introduced their own in the past few years.

Cycling on a hire bike is often the simplest and most enjoyable way to get around a city... Paris's velib system is superb, and has come accompanied by excellent bicycle lanes that wind around the French capital. An undergound train/metro system leaves you with no concept of the layout and sights of a city, and public transport can be expensive and unfamiliar. Arm yourself with a good map, though, and stick to bike lanes where you can find them. It goes without saying that you should check the local road conventions (at the very least) – get on the right (or left) side of the road.

What to look for in a biking bag

While it's possible to cycle around with supermarket bags hanging off your handlebars, using a decent bag to cycle with can transform the experience completely.

• Your best options are either a good quality rucksack or an across-the-body bag like the ones cycle couriers use. Make sure the straps are padded and comfortable – vintage leather rucksacks and satchels often have hard straps that will rub when riding.

• Look for something as lightweight as possible. It's suprising what can feel heavy after twenty minutes perched on your shoulders.

• Bags with a strap or patch of wicking at the front for attaching lights will give you extra visibility when riding in the evenings.

• If you cycle long distances, find a bag with a separate compartment for your cycle gear. Otherwise everything in your bag will become dank and a bit sweaty.

• When using a courier bag, make sure you switch shoulders every time you ride, so you don't strain one part of your back.

• Go for something long or deep enough to house a lightweight pump. They're notorious for slipping out if not properly contained.

Chapter 6

Bike Maintenance

For **bike maintenance**, like tuning gears or replacing brakes, it really is best to throw money at the problem. Think of self-repairs as you would a car. Replacing a tyre is just about do-able; fitting new brakes is probably **more of a challenge** than you're ready for, with a **big fall-out if you mess it up.**

Essential kit

Bike kits should contain all of these items:

- A pump that fits your valves; they are not all the same! The best have gauges and look a bit like dynamite plungers from cartoons, but you can't carry them round with you.

- Puncture patches – these are a bit like plasters. But much tougher, so Mickey Mouse elastoplasts will not suffice.

- Rubber vulcanising solution. Otherwise known as glue.

- A small piece of fine oilpaper or sandpaper.

- A piece of chalk to mark your puncture. Lipstick also works – but you won't want to be wearing it again afterwards.

- Tyre levers, or spanners. Ideally three: they're used to lever off your tyre.

- A spare inner tube: the best money you'll ever spend.

- Disposable plastic gloves: not essential, but good to have.

Below are the jobs that a bike novice should be able to handle quite easily.

Fix a puncture/flat tyre

To be honest, puncture repairs are cheap at a bike shop, so if you're nervous or in a hurry, go easy on yourself and let someone do the hard work for you. However, if you're on a budget or miles from a bike shop, and in possession of all the essential kit, here's how to fix your hole.

Firstly, riding with a spare inner tube (the balloon-like, inflated hoop that sits inside your tyre) in your bike kit will be a great relief if you ever get a puncture on the road as it makes for a quick fix.

If you have an inner tube, follow steps 1 to 7. If you don't (fool!) follow steps 1 to 4, then move to 8. Do not pass Go. Do not collect £200!

1. Stand your bike upside down and undo your tyre. On some bikes there will be a quick release lever in the centre of the wheel, on others you'll have to use the little alum key from your repair kit or a spanner to undo the bolt in the wheel. If it's a back wheel it gets a bit more complicated. You'll need to pull back on the rear derailleur, then lower your wheel down between the brake pads, then forward slightly to clear the chain and the derailleur. NB If you have a rear-wheel puncture on a bike with gears, put it into the lowest gear (i.e. the easiest one to pedal on) first as this makes it easier to reposition the wheel.

2. Once you have the wheel off your bike, you need to get your inner tube out from under the wheel using a spanner or tyre levers from your kit. You basically wedge a spanner or lever between the metal and the tyre, and lever a section of tyre out. Then you do the same thing a few centimetres along until the whole thing is loose. After the first couple of sections it gets much easier.

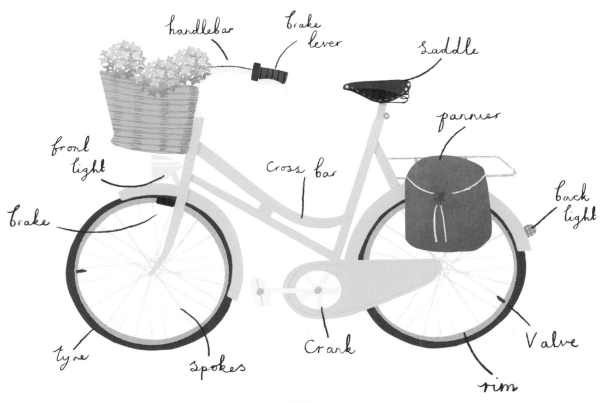

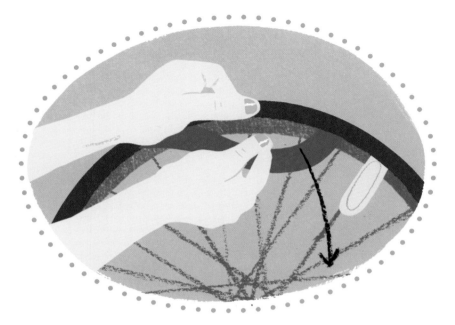

3. Don't make the common mistake of pulling the tyre off completely; just lever off one side of it, section by section, and you should be able to access the inner tube and pull it out. That way it's a bit easier to get the tyre back on afterwards.

4. While you're working on dislodging one side of the tyre, pump up the flaccid inner tube a little bit so you can hear a hissing from where the air is escaping. This tells you where your puncture is. This is really important: if there's still a bit of glass stuck in your tyre, it will end up re-puncturing your newly repaired/replaced inner tube, and a few metres down the road you'll be in the same crappy boat. Find the offending object and pull it out with haste.

5. If you're using a spare inner tube, you can just deflate and pack away the punctured one here, partially inflate your new one, and prod it back under the tyre, starting with the valve and working your way around.

6. Now use your levers or spanners to lever back in the loose side of the tyre, starting at the valve and working around it. When you get to the final portion it will be quite hard work – a tip is to use two of your levers to keep the far ends of the loose portion in place, and then lever the centre portion in with a third spanner/lever.

7. Finally, inflate your tyre in full and replace the dust-caps (the little lids on the valves). Whoopeeee.

8. If you don't have a spare inner tube, you can patch up your inner tube fairly easily.
   - First of all, pump your duff tube right up to find out where the hole is. You should be able to hear air escaping, even on a slow puncture. If you can't, try to find a bucket of water to plunge it into: you'll see bubbles where the hole is.
   - Use the bit of chalk in your repair kit, or even lipstick, to mark the hole.
   - Smooth the area around the hole with sandpaper, then wipe it down and cover it with a layer of glue about the size of a coin. Leave until it's nearly dry; just tacky.
   - Press your patch over the hole, and smooth down so there are no bubbles on the surface. Leave to dry for ten minutes, and perhaps spend the time ruminating on how much easier all this would have been with a spare inner tube. Go back to step 5 above and think about what you've done.

Check tyre pressure

Tyres, unless they're really old and rubbish, should indicate the recommended pressure on the side. It will be between 60–80 for a mountain bike, and 80–100 for something with skinny wheels.

1. Remove the dust caps (the little lids on the valves) and slot the pump over it.

2. If you're using a proper gauge pump (the ones that look like dynamite plungers from cartoons), you'll be able to see what the pressure of your tyre is as you pump. Remove the dust caps, then pump up the tyres. Keep pumping until you reach the correct pressure.

3. Pull the pump off – don't worry about air escaping as the valves should stop this happening as soon as you release them.

4. Screw the dust caps back on.

If you don't have a valve pump, just keep pumping until your tyres are really, really hard and it's getting tough to pump any more. And start saving for a decent pump!

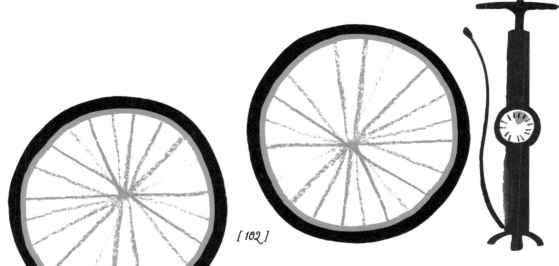

Replace handlebar tape

This one is easy and quickly improves the appearance of your bike. Incidentally, if your tape is a bit grubby rather than in a state of total disrepair, wiping it over with some oven cleaner works a treat.

You will need:
- A handlebar tape kit
- Decent scissors
- A scouring pad or scrubber

1. Take off the little lids at the end of your handlebars.
2. Pull back the hoods which might cover the start of your brakes.
3. Unwrap and discard your old tape.
4. Give the surface a good scrub to get rid of grimy traces of glue and other unpleasantries.
5. There should be two short pieces of tape about ten centimetres long in your kit. Use them to tape over the rings which fasten your brakes to your handlebars; the awkward corner bit. They should be self-adhesive. If they're not, fasten them with black tape. If you can't find these shorter pieces, just cut some from the full-length tape.
6. Your kit should have two long rolls of tape. Use one per side. Starting at the end of your handlebar, wrap the tape around and around, towards the centre of the handlebars. Overlap each new layer slightly on top of the last – about one centimetre.
7. At the end of the roll, secure with pieces of glossy tape, which should come as part of your kit.
8. Pop the caps back on at the end of the handlebars and you're done.

Sort out tyres that rub on your brake

1. Lift the bike off the ground and spin the wheels. If the rubbing is slight, you'll be able to fix it by adjusting the brake alignment screw. Don't worry, this excruciatingly boring-sounding process is actually simple. Look for a screw that is on the brake where it touches the wheel (see diagram A).

2. Turn the screw in either direction, until the brake no longer rubs the wheel when you spin it. A little turn should be enough to sort out the rub.

3. If the rub is quite heavy, then you might need to adjust the cable itself. Use a spanner to adjust the nut which attaches the brake cable to the brake. Release a little bit of cable, then tighten the nut again.

4. Give the wheel a little spin to test for rubbing again, and adjust accordingly. Squeeze the brake lever a few times to be sure the new slack in the cable has reached the brake. Loosen the cable further if necessary.

Tighten loose brakes

1. If you look closely, you'll see that just in front of the brake handle on your handlebars is a little screw adjuster which the brake cable goes through. If you turn it anti-clockwise, you will shorten your brakes a bit, making them tighter and stronger.

2. When you pull your brakes, you shouldn't be able to pull them right back to the handlebar. If you can, keep turning that little screw adjuster until you can't (see diagram B).

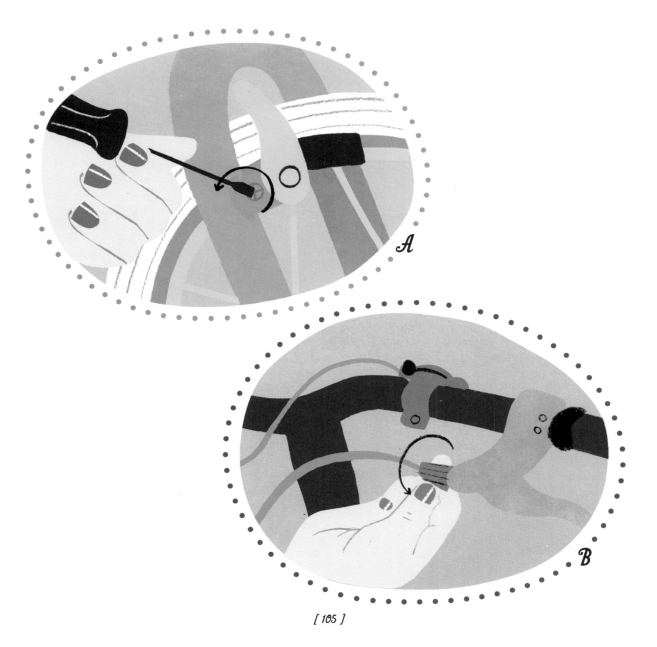

Tips for general good upkeep

The best way to minimise the cost of your bike upkeep is to tinker with it a little and often. Keep a little bottle of bike grease (available at all bike stores) wherever you keep your bike, and try to dribble a bit on your chain while turning it with the pedal, whenever you remember – about once a fortnight. You'll need to do this outside as you don't want this stuff on your carpets. You should also oil the cranks and gears, anywhere where there is friction. But do this no more often than fortnightly, as otherwise it pools and attracts dirt, which in turn clogs up your cogs.

Unfortunately, it's not enough just to add layer upon layer of lubrication without also giving your bike chain a bit of a clean once in a while. If you leave lubricant to accumulate, it will eventually become an abrasive, filled with nasty bits of grit and dirt that will erode your lovely chain, and make riding a noisy struggle.

Take an old toothbrush to clean the nooks and crannies, using a (widely available) solvent. It's easier if you take it portion by portion, looping it off the bracket. In all honesty, this is a grotty, boring job and a chain is one of the cheapest bits on your bike. If you can spare a bit of money every few months, just buy a new one.

Keep your tyres at the correct pressure at all times. If you don't, you can self-cause punctures when the inner tube gets bundled up with your floppy tyre. More on this on page 102.

Many bike shops will fit anti-puncture tape between the tyre and the inner tube for you. It's a quick and cheap way to prolong the life of your wheels.

If you can afford them, buy strong anti-puncture tyres like Armadillos. These should pay for themselves long term, outlasting standard tyres by a mile and saving a packet on inner tubes – not to mention the anguish of the roadside puncture, the blight of all cyclists.

Park your bike somewhere sheltered to prevent rust from rain and precipitation.

Check your bike for chips every few weeks. Any gaps in the paintwork can be painted over with clear nail varnish to prevent rust.

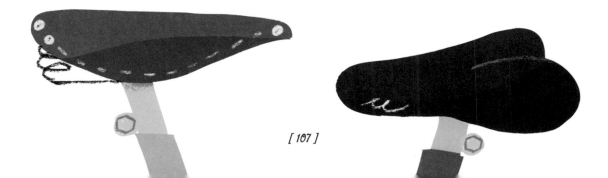

Resources

United Kingdom

Bikeability (www.bikeability.org.uk)
Cycling Proficiency for the twenty-first century
CTC (www.ctc.org)
Political lobbying organisation that also offers insurance and legal assistance
Cycle Training UK (www.cycletraining.co.uk)
Provides cycle training
LCC (www.lcc.org.uk)
Organisation promoting cycling in London
Sustrans (www.sustrans.org.uk)
Pushes for safe cycle routes

Australia

Bicycles Network Australia (www.bicycles.net.au/links/orgs.html)
Australian cycling organisations and bicycle user groups

Bike Paths & Rail Trails (www.bikepaths.com.au/)
Online store and comprehensive guide to bike trails and maps, cycling health and safety, and bike shops

Handbook for Bicycle Riders (www.bicycleinfo.nsw.gov.au/downloads/bicycle_riders_handbook.pdf)
Plain-English downloadable handbook for cyclists, approved by the NSW Roads and Traffic Authority (RSA)

USA

Cyclecraft (www.cyclecraft.co.org)
The definitive guide to cycling safely

New York City Dot (www.nyc.gov/)
Information on cyling in New York

Bicycling Street Smarts (www.bikexprt.com/streetsmarts/usa/index.htm)
Online booklet aimed at increasing your safety and confidence on the roads

Bike Commute Tips (bikecommutetips.blogspot.com/)
Tips on commuting to work on your bike

Cool blogs

http://bikesnobnyc.blogspot.com/
http://www.copenhagencyclechic.com/
http://londoncyclechic.blogspot.com/

Index

First published in 2012 by Hardie Grant Books

Hardie Grant Books UK
Dudley House, North Suite
34–35 Southampton Street
London WC2E 7HF
www.hardiegrant.co.uk

Hardie Grant Books (Australia)
Ground Floor, Building 1
658 Church Street
Melbourne, VIC 3121
www.hardiegrant.com.au

British Library Cataloguing-in-Publication Data.
A catalogue record for this book is available
from the British Library.

ISBN 978-1-74270-255-1

Commissioning Editor: Kate Pollard
Cover and internal design: Nikki Parkes
Editor: Nicky Jeanes
Text: Katie Dailey
Illustrations: Clare Owen
Index: Marian Anderson
Colour reproduction: by MDP
Printed and bound in China by 1010 Printing International Limited

10 9 8 7 6 5 4 3 2 1